NATIONAL ANTHEM

I0211828

Mohamed Hassan is an award-winning journalist and author from Auckland and Cairo whose poetry is taught in schools internationally. He was the 2015 New Zealand National Poetry Slam Champion and placed second at the 2021 UK National Slam. His essay collection *How To Be A Bad Muslim* (Penguin, 2022) was nominated for a National Heritage Award, and his Sky TV comedy series *Miles From Nowhere* was released in 2024 to critical acclaim. He dreams about the Nile.

Also by Mohamed Hassan

How To Be A Bad Muslim   (Penguin Random House, 2022)

CONTENTS

IV.

© 2025, Mohamed Hassan. All rights reserved. No part of this book may be reproduced, stored in a retrieval system, or transmitted in any form or by any means, whether electronic, mechanical, photocopying, recording, or otherwise, without the prior written permission of the publisher, except in the case of brief quotations used in reviews or scholarly works.

This work may not be used for text and data mining, including (without limitation) the training of artificial intelligence technologies or systems. The author and publisher expressly reserve all rights and opt out of any applicable text and data mining exceptions.

ISBN: 978-1-917617-43-7

Cover designed by Aaron Kent

Typeset by Aaron Kent

The author has asserted their right to be identified as the author of this Work in accordance with the Copyright, Designs and Patents Act 1988

Broken Sleep Books Ltd
PO BOX 102
Llandysul
SA44 9BG

National Anthem

Mohamed Hassan

Broken Sleep Books

كله سلف ودين حتى المشي على الرجلين

Everything is borrowed and lent, even walking on this earth

— Teta

WHEN THEY ASK YOU WHERE YOU ARE (REALLY) FROM

Tell them

you are an unrequited pilgrim

two parallel lives that never touch

a whisper or a window

to what your country could be

if only it opened its arms

and took you whole

tell them about the moon

how she eats at your skin

watches you pray and fast and cry

while the world sleeps

how she gives birth to herself and dies

and you wish upon her children

how you wander her night

plant cardamom in your friends' eyes

cumin in their teeth

zaatar on their brow

lick the rest off your fingertips

it tastes of visa-on-entry

heaven with no random checks

round the iftar table everyone speaks

of politics and God

trans rights and colonialism

we forget we didn't speak the empire's tongue

                                                            once

BIRD PRAYER

I was not born a forest
burning against the night

not a flower hitchhiking
along the seasons

before I bloomed
a watered bud

dug fingernails from earth
to dance in the sun

before the soil I left
in search of foreign fields

before growth, before beat
before life and just after the Spring

between bones and ash I was born

a single hope

a future unwritten

BURY ME

All of my recurring dreams
take place in my grandfather's flat

they hang around with the ghosts
sticking to the shelves

they drip from the long neon bulbs

my dad hung me out to dry
in front of the whole family

said I hadn't been raised right

I cried because I wanted Amr's rocket ship
and not my blue sippy cup

I don't know why this still lives here
22 years after my grandfather died

he's still there framed next to the windowsill
the armchair and laptop and my grandmother's   voice

we taught her how to play *Fayza Ahmed*
on YouTube and abandoned her frantically

trying to shut it down when his song came on

she pressed all the keys and then sat
in her tears until one of us showed up

when the Lebanese talk of love they say   *to'borny*
a prayer to never have to bury the one you love

that they should be the one to dig your grave
and plant flowers and live with the memory

you can't discard a loss the way you can
a birthday gift or a broken laptop

it lives with you, sleeps in the spare room
by the laundry and occasionally eats your food

I want to never lose my parents
but find a loss like that in someone

a love that sears into your lungs and lingers
if you draw the short straw and not die first

JOHN LENNON

People talk about John Lennon like he was God

                but he never spoke to me

the songs I breathe to
make my bones ache
smell like mama's deep
fried cauliflower after
a long day of diaspora

Mohamed Fouad sings

            I still remember you   فاكرك

            the one who forgot me   يا ناسيني

and I am sweating
guilt a homeland I have
sewn onto my palms
but can't dream in hold
my arabic between
my knees

my grandfather scolded

me_____for/

_____stutterin/

through/_____the/_____Quran/

but my mother taught me

Allah blesses every failure

it doesn't taste as sweet

when it comes easy

I unbutton english grammar

but daydream of not having

a tumored mother tongue

tumbling over the weight

of expectation

when Umm Kalthoum shakes

her handkerchief wildly

in the air it's rude

not to stare she drinks

her arabic like sex

or a violin string licking

its bow from chin to elbow

They spoke to me about you again   كلموني تاني عنك

____I remember_____   فكروني

_____I remember   فكروني

hold out your open hands

for deliverance, the moans

on the live recordings

from 1940s audience

disciples are every part

the composition

this woman

a planet

this history

orbiting with her

our hands flailing

in the glory of an earth

created to birth her millions

of years of evolution leading to

the moment the orchestra quiets

and a messenger speaks her first *ahh*   آه

swelling like a red dwarf through time and

space and me on an unsuspecting Thursday

afternoon in a shisha lounge a 24 hour

flight from the hospital I was born in

and it shouldn't hurt this much

to love a country that does

not love you back

that no longer has a place for you

in its dazzling future that would trap

you in its claws and stigmata you a traitor

and what Beatles song could ever

make me feel that way

THE MOTHER OF THE WORLD

Only Arabs would care so much about appearances
they'd have a second lounge with plastic wrapping
you'd get a smack if you sat on it without permission
God help you if you spilt food

my uncle tells me I've romanticised Egypt
he can't understand why I'm not content
with Western opportunities kids my age
fling themselves into the open sea just to taste

a smugglers boat at 2am is not the same
as an economy class ticket but we are running
from the same beast
to the same beast

when *my country my country* plays we both feel
the same pang of longing
the same pang of disgust

> one sign of trauma
> is *dissociation*:

[feeling distant from your own
body, your reflection a series of
collapsing memories kept in a
china teapot you open when guests
arrive]

Kareem sends me a message
on January 25 every year without fail

                    [don't worry ya basha
                    the thawra continues]

Khaled pitches me two stories a day
about young activists, lawyers, kids
with eyes bigger than their stomachs
thrown into a cell for talking about the sun

if he closes his eyes he can see his friends
falling from sniper fire in Tahrir and Ramses and Rabaa

he smiles from ear to ear
and you can't see it in his eyes

                    one sign of trauma
                    is *hyper-association*:

[connecting everything back to a
single moment]

I pass an open sewer in Brixton markets

and I am back outside my grandfather's

flat, the jasmine trees croaking beneath

the circus balloon, watching my parents

fall in love, the secret police arrest my cousin

the sweat on Abdelhalim's forehead

before he collapses on stage

for the last time

وان لقاكم حبيبي سلمولي عليه

if you ever meet the one I love

send him my regards

طمنوني الاسمراني عاملة ايه الغربة

فيه

tell me about his golden skin

what diaspora has done to him

AND BEFORE THAT WE WERE STARS

Can you please look at this poem
and tell me if it's good?

it's for my fiancé she's really far away
I want to say how I feel
but my English is limited, can you read it?

she works retail most nights
closes up shop late and I can't study anymore
since my mother moved back to Yemen
I am working six days a week driving buses
I want to make her feel special, you know?

she'll be here in two months
and we've been stretching words like this
four years making bridges out of paper
folded like passports
                          like sailboats

                                        floating into the sky

have you ever tried to fold
your heart into an envelope?

she's got a green card and works most days
and lives in North Carolina

we skype and I read her poems

the sentences crack her eyes whisper

you're a poet you believe in eternal love right?

last night she was here

we didn't sleep crying

the travel document they gave her

at the border is expiring

are they going to let her back in?

they won't let us stay in New Zealand

she has no passport

will they let me into America?

we were born in different refugee camps

but walk past the train tracks

in Morningside and remember the same smell

the curtain air the turquoise governments

perched on our shoulders waiting

does that count as a visa?

can you build a house out of love

if there is no soil?

but what if we never do?

VERTIGO

I spend hours

watching the tips

of skyscrapers

office blocks

libraries

        anything more

        than four stories high

outside the councillor's office

through thick glass

        I sit

        watching

there is a beautiful abduction

about reinforced concrete beams

thousands of tiny steel rods

shooting up

        a ladder at a pool's edge

            a diving board

a glossy poster from the 90s

watches with us

our shared she'll be right

won't work

it whispers

with practiced concern

somewhere behind my ears

the siren folds its arms

you know I don't like it

when you talk to strangers

OFFICE CHRISTMAS PARTY

All my life I've wanted to fit in and never have

like a hippopotamus at an office Christmas party

who doesn't drink for religious reasons

no one knows what to do with me

small talk feels like root canal

I am bored by my own existence

waking up a premature birth

work a doomsday bunker

I didn't choose to survive with you people

no I didn't watch the rugby

no I don't care about your boat

or your children

those who really know me call me asshole

my politeness an act of professional avoidance

a canary singing in my throat

boredom has paved me into the darkest places

it is more satisfying to fantasise

unspeakable violence against myself and others

than fend this gravity alone

here's what none of the pamphlets

 at the university health clinic tell you:

the path of least resistance is self-loathing

you can't see your value when the lights are out

if you hold everyone at arm's length

you never have to apologise

or ask for help

HEAVEN IS A WINDOW YOU CAN CLIMB THROUGH

From the top of the Sky-
Tower we watch lovers
uncouple against

the sunset, red and screaming
light across faces of buildings
unbent by time, everyone belts

romance and the band plays over-
produced pop songs, a girl weeps
in disbelief, a boyfriend begs her

to calm down, two strangers long
for each other's bones, a boy made
of scruff dances for every lost

night of wild, his heart unnerved, a hurt
like a heaven on his chest, we eat burgers
by the wharf, I make conversation

with people I'd rather not, practice my best
fake smile, the train smells like the morning
after, the earth is a flat plane, an endless reel

spinning on a loop, what if I never leave?

II.

it must be somewhere in your bloodline

WHEN THEY TELL YOU TO GO BACK TO WHERE YOU CAME FROM

Tell them about the moon

how she eats at your skin

watches you pray and fast and cry

while the world sleeps

how she gives birth to herself and dies

and you wish upon her children

how you wander her night

plant cardamom in your friends' eyes

cumin in their teeth

zaatar on their brow

lick the rest off your fingertips

it tastes of visa-on-entry

heaven with no random checks

round the iftar table everyone speaks

of politics and God

trans rights and colonialism

we forget we didn't speak the empire's tongue

once

THE CYST

In the small of my back
at the edge of where my fingertips reach
when I stretch them over my shoulder
is a dream of one day going back home for good

it's a tiny dream
small enough that I can hide it in a knot
slipped under the slight fracture in my lower spine
the one the back surgeon told me not to worry about
but that once in a batch in Samoa
was in so much pain I thought
I would be paralysed

now I do core exercises at the gym
and use the foam roller
and it doesn't bother me as much

I've tried to teach myself to be less idealistic as I've gotten older
to think more about interest rates
and less about post-colonial struggles
my KiwiSaver account can't do much for restoring social equality in Egypt
but it could help me put down a deposit for a house in Whangarei

if the housing market crashes and I get a raise

I read somewhere that back problems don't actually get better

you're kinda stuck with them for life

but you can keep it from getting worse if you're careful

the surgeon said it was true

he also said the X-rays found a large cyst

pushing up against my spine that had been growing since I was a kid

slowly where no one could see it

it hurts every once in a while

when I hear my grandma's voice or listen to a Fouad song

and for a second I can smell the cold cement floor

and the jasmines in the window

the hum of static off the glass of our ninth story flat

but I do some back extensions and stretch my upper hamstrings

and the pain passes

the surgeon says I shouldn't worry about it

that the cyst looks bad on the scans but is harmless

a lot of people carry them around all their lives and it's fine

I just gotta bend my knees when I lift heavy boxes or watch the news

I told him I was relieved

but a small part of me really wanted the surgery

RACIST IS NOT A SLUR

But by God would they

make you believe it is

cracking their feet

and bulging their teeth

eyes rinsing

a thousand self-beliefs

the goats will crow at dawn

and the bulls will run through the sewers

and you will be told to shut up

and have some respect

do you know

what I have mourned

                                        for you people

how dare you scratch your nails

across this flag

how dare you gargle

at the hand that breeds

that took you in

when no one would

did we not bathe you

in our mercy

did we not dry you

with our tolerance

did you not smile

and wave

at the citizenship ceremony

and promise to be good

                    and grateful

                              and quiet

EVERYBODY LOVES A BAD MUSLIM

A jaded jihadi
a sun-kissed antagonist
unwashed beard
veins popping
yelling at a television crew
in a developing country

his poor teenage wife
covered from head-to-toe in fear
wide eyes
calling from the shadows

but I have not woken up for fajr prayer
in six months

stopped speaking Allah's name
before I eat

forgot to ask about halal certificate
at the new burger place next door

got angry at a man my father's age on the train
for not getting out fast enough when my stop arrived

TO FALLEN ANGELS DRAGGED FROM WINDOW SEATS
for Dr. David Dao

One day we will evolve to stretch the skin out

from our backs to make wings

meet our loved ones at sea

embrace under clear skies no government owns

today I hug my western passport and pray

there is enough colour in my aisle

to keep us all safe

out of inconvenience

WELCOME TO PARADISE

He says as we're led
into the questioning room
the other guards snigger

we are all Arabs and Asians
there are no phones allowed
no sense of time

but a San Francisco video plays
on an endless loop

there are no more *sirs*, no

thank you for flying with us today

in this room, it's

how much money do you have
I said turn off your phone
we can send you back anytime we want

the golden gates shimmer
like pearls in the California sun

and we are waiting
for our names to be called

CUSTOMS: A LOVE STORY

Dear airport customs officer,

I know you want me

I saw you staring from across the terminal
that dark look in your eyes.
a hunger you don't quite understand

maybe it's the way my name
swirls around your tongue
my olive skin
my eyes piercing through
the grainy passport photo

you tell me it's random, but I know
the moment our eyes locked
you couldn't wait to get your hands on me

to strip me down
to search through my luggage

I don't have much
but I'll share it with you

I'm not saying I ain't flattered

(I am!)

getting chosen out of all these people

watching their jealous sneers

as I'm lead down the aisle

and into the questioning room

harsh lights and cold seats

(it's the way I always dreamed it would be)

you have so many questions

where did I grow up?

am I single?

have I ever been part

of an international terrorist syndicate?

(This is all moving so fast!)

listen

let's take things slow

I want this, I do

but let's build a relationship

on more than just racial profiling

I want you to know the *real* me

can't you see that I

well…

I'm just a boy

standing in front of a boy

asking him

to let me in

IT'S BEEN 48 HOURS SINCE I LAST SAW A WHITE PERSON

And it's not like I feel any more familiar
cannonballed into a world that doesn't
speak my tongues

I've been throwing myself into spaces
I didn't belong since puberty, my presence
a tiny rebellion to every

go back to where we colonised you

and it's not like my government
didn't warn me against being in Istanbul

you can still smell the shrapnel and trauma
in Ortakoy, the tear gas and neoliberalism
in Taksim, a nation stretching itself and
trying to be everyone at once

and it's not like I haven't thought about
where I would go when the next one hits
what hospital I would find when I didn't know
the emergency number, the word for help
in Turkish

but I walk down Istiklal's open mouth
the air a flurry of megaphones and oud
watch lovers kiss each others' hands
as if it's all they ever wanted to do

and I realise no one has asked me where
I'm from, and when they did it was warm
and kind and not distant and not waiting

for a chance to snap and not watching me
from the corner of their eye and not wishing
me theirs and not yellow smiling polite
and mirrorless

and for a second I feel safe
like a home or a book you can see yourself
                                        inside of

LIFE AT A DISTANCE

My father came to this country

with a master's degree

and a fist full of English

he doesn't talk about that time

but my mother does

she tells us she prayed he would

not find work so she'd never leave

my grandma, her sisters, the nine

floors she had to climb while pregnant

every day before they installed

the elevator to our apartment

she doesn't tell us about the stares

the kids yelling after her when she

dropped us off at school

the woman who told her to get

the hell back to where you came from

in the Milford Mall carpark

the nights she cried in our single bathroom

twenty years later I land in Istanbul
with a Postgraduate degree
and a fist full of Turkish

suddenly all my learned assimilation
means nothing, the kiwiness I fought
tooth and nail for is strange

I catch the stares at the grocer's
watch taxi drivers puff at my broken pleas

migration is its own form
of social isolation

an ocean that sits between you
and everyone else

a distance you must swim everyday
just to make it to the starting line

there are nights when loneliness
strikes and the walls are caving in

when your friends are in a different time zone
and WhatsApp messages can't make up for physical touch

but you sleep it off, you walk through the city
for hours, listen to 10,000 podcasts, practice
your Turkish at the supermarket, skype
your mum and she tells you off for not calling her

                                                    enough

and you realise she is wading through
her own migration, that like her
you are a dandelion flung in the wind

landing in strange places and planting
roots where you can

my mother skypes grandma every morning
watches Egyptian soap operas on her ipad

but she doesn't want to leave this country now

her garage where she teaches toddlers Arabic
the weekly lessons at the mosque, the English
she spent twenty years learning and relearning

the flea market my father buys her flowers from

on Sundays, the way the Pacific sun skims

off the balcony and opens up the living room

she tells me she is praying

that I come home

and home

by any other name

                                is a quarantine

                                you have chosen

is a field of dandelions

flung together

                                learning to grow

III.

which parts have you stolen

WHEN THEY ASK YOU WHY YOU SPEAK SO WELL FOR AN IMMIGRANT

Tell them

about your grandmother's laugh

how you never quite knew whether she was story or myth

the upper lip in your conviction

or a song ringing in your bones

drifting through the kitchen window

with the fried shrimp and newspaper voodoo dolls

tell them how you have always been a voodoo doll

your feet licking the flames

the stove top eye a television screen

a news bulletin

an open casket

the needle pushing and pulling through your skin

every puncture a question played by an accusation

every bullet hole an answer you have to fill

           with silence

           with religion

           with Xanax and daytime television

I'D LIKE TO RENEGOTIATE MY RETIREMENT CONTRIBUTIONS

I am not the harbinger of doom
I am just a journalist

I wake up and stare
into the mouldy armpit of human existence
so you don't have to

flat white in hand, report back my findings

yes,

> young men with eyes like horizons are still drowning in
> the Mediterranean

yes,

> limited-edition retro Air Force One's might come with air
> pockets but not health insurance for wholesale interns in
> Bangladesh

yes,

> that early morning nausea you feel after coffee is just the
> lack of oxygen from hamburger farms in the Amazon

most days I am flying frantic

howling at the sun

beaching myself onto your timeline

with the grace of engine failure

        studies have shown

        all our stars are now dead

        and we have been wishing

        upon ourselves

but we are just as burning

just as drifting

lost in our brilliance

to notice the worlds

we are swallowing

and am I too a star

rising through the ashes

a false profit sent by the gods

to birth the world in their image

a sexy new type of woke jester

to sing and flail

my people my people

look at the mess we have made

how barbar and terror and ugly we pray

wishing for a scent

of progress

and I will return to the office

passport in hand and a story to sell

a noble savage with a student loan

a gladiator plucked from poverty

to dance among the rich

THERE ARE BOMBS OVER GAZA AGAIN, ARE YOU WATCHING?

I don't like the post even though I'm tagged
in it, today I am witless on a bus to meet a soul
mate who isn't, in the most liveable city that
isn't, wearing Nikes despite my best intentions

hey, they're anti-Trump but pro-sweatshops, it's
five o'clock and I'm on the wrong bus home, the
cars pile up to flee the free market's spleen, thank
god it's Friday but the bombs are still dropping

on a Palestine that isn't, I am a reporter but feel
silent, making news about house prices and a US
president that isn't, talking about a Muslim ban
that isn't, I am a Muslim on a bus leaving Auckland

and I'm trying not to read the news, talk to friends
in Denver who pray in terminals not made for our
skin and I tweet about Kanye and check my follows
check my new shoes in the glass waiting for the

wrong bus, I wear Palestinian colours by accident
and no one notices, wear a beard by accident

and hope I don't have to travel soon, watch the

skyline shrink and thank god for a hot meal

and Netflix, for a soulmate at a bus stop in a home that

isn't, I don't think about Israeli jets ruffling the nights

feathers, I don't think about when my life is ending

I don't think about where I'll meet my soulmate

if my house is bombed, if my car explodes, if they build

walls in our living rooms and we have to hold hands

through the cracks, if we never see each other again

because of a security policy, though a part of me wonders

if it would make breaking up easier

WHERE ARE YOU, SUPERMOON?

Last night the moon clawed at everything

the earth rattled its spine

the wind barked through teeth

not to be outdone

the rivers turned their banks

the streets bleeding rain

and I woke up late for work

my body its own list of demands

BY THE BOSPHORUS STRAIT I SAT DOWN AND WEPT

Breathe in.

When Istanbulites woke up to find the water a bright turquoise they thought the worst. A curse had taken over the city or toxins seeped from textile factories. But scientists agreed it was just an explosion of plankton migrating from the Black Sea, a milky blessing heralding the summer calm. I am told it's serene.

Breathe out.

I did not find out I was colour blind until they tested our class at the library in Form 2. It explained so much. Why I always coloured grass in brown and tree bark green. Why I'd clash my outfits and no one is impolite enough to tell me. My parents must have thought I was stupid or acting out. The scientists agreed it was neither.

Breathe in.

My manager told me that things can be difficult here, but when you walk along the Bosphorous it makes it all worth it. Sometimes I think this city is magical. Other times I'm sure it is cursed. A dark pact signed in its catacombs centuries ago threatening to explode. Most of the time it is sad, mourning a lover lost or a friend it couldn't save.

Breathe out.

Every day at 12.30pm I walk out of the office and stand at its chin waiting for a sign, the air to return, the explosions to subside. But the panic attacks are a calendar event, barging into a meeting room, a hungry mall, a dolmus packed with strangers and I tense my abdomen and squeeze my shirt with my hands and try not to remember.

For the life of me all I can see is blue. Even the scientists are at a loss on this one. They tell me to relax my shoulders and focus on my breathing. Not worry about time I can't unwind.

It's amazing how something can be right in front of you and you just can't see it.

GRIEF IS AN EXPENSIVE HABIT

My work hooked me up with the company therapist a week after
Yasmine died

who broke down listening to the story, told me to imagine I am a
character
in a Turkish soap, my fate written by committee, the drama
dragged out
to fill a three hour Friday night slot with ad breaks and one hell
                                                    of a cliff hanger

if I watched the characters from behind a television screen trying
to prevent
a catastrophe that was already written would it make me feel
more, or less, in control

the second therapist told me to read The Alchemist, asked me how
my parents
conditioned me into emotional detachment, whether my multiple
bathroom breaks
were a sign of avoidance

I am a poet who writes about my feelings but can't open up with-
out being in character
without the stage lights and orange diffusers softening my face for
the audience

the third made me take my shoes off at the door and wear shower caps

over my socks, his office smelled like whisky and divorce

it's amazing the kind of help you can afford as an expat living through

someone else's recession, I bought the best drugs and slept through my youth

the last one said I was an emptied vial of strength swirling around a bathtub drain

that every calamity was an opportunity to grow, a teething seed after a bushfire

so maybe I'm not the volunteer firefighter

maybe I'm just the neighbourhood dog

chasing the fire truck

                              not knowing where it's headed

TINY GRAVEYARDS

It is too cold outside to dream

instead I sink into a couch

made of motherland

fold pastries into my mouth

afloat in a dry house

if I close my eyes and twist my fingers in the air

my life is a highlight reel

I rewind the best parts

colour grade the madness

pay homage to the greats

my mistakes look beautiful in slow motion

my regrets nonchalant with a laughing track

when I was eighteen the world was a straight line

a series of long days and short nights

but slowly I am learning to rot

to love the strange men I was created after

it would be a waste to fight this now

and the angels would die

to lick the burning from our lungs

they will swindle us

with flight and grace

but we will never let go

we will run under dubious skies

paint murals of our fathers

                                    and overthrow them

fade out when we have dug

our beds and watered them

a ritual of sleep, a pair of white lips

smiling under a screaming sun

TINY EARTHQUAKES

and maybe an abyss of delicate chaos
is just a sign of life

and maybe sirens into an open sky
is a season breathing again

and maybe the sleeping motorways
are a daydream we had once

a world in which we could run
and run and run

and maybe sitting alone in your thoughts
is the only way to know which parts of you

                                        are real

and maybe a well of unused words
could water a family tree

and maybe self-love is a boxing match
with no rules

just blood and broken teeth and glory

today the sky rested

its head on my shoulders

and there was laughter in my bones

I am a foraging elk in a wildfire

I will outlive, a friend to the growth spurts

dressed as demons

a kissing sun, a delicate earth

a life worth ending and beginning

CHASING/BORDERS

I am a copper pot full of dreams, all handles and no mouth

you are a fire. or a hammer.

the day I meet you the Prozac is circling above the smog
the melancholy a city of sleepless lights

death's stomach growls and we blow orange shisha rings
and talk art, talk Himalayas and I think about tiny words again

my neck wraps around your hands and we awkward dance
in the lobby of a restaurant we can't afford
a sleepy town with no one watching the stars

the mammoth between us brought to his knees for a night
or two, a stray weekend, our eyes a tangle of sleep

you see me in a way that makes me think more of myself
it is a new thought, a breeze that lifts my arms and soars

we are full of good food, I am folded laundry, you are full lips and
no secrets

we sow moments together and make a blanket, stretch time
around our bones, say nothing significant

I am weighed down by what I couldn't carry
you are zoning out in the middle of conversations

the city looks the other way and we steal her children
set them into the ocean, each a dancing lantern
a house of trinkets from Seoul and Moscow and Paris

you are more sentimental than you let on
I am learning to be bold

together we will paint something maybe no one has seen before
a hot flash in a pining world, a train station we will meet and part
and meet and part until we can tie our feet to each other for good

or great

IV.

this beautiful

WHEN THEY TELL YOU THEY ARE SORRY

The muazzen calls you to pray

on the radio

you wrap your limbs

in cotton sheets

walk through the crowd

with your hands

in your mouth

                                                    waiting for the gun

WHITE SUPREMACY IS A SONG WE ALL KNOW THE WORDS TO BUT NEVER SING OUT LOUD

Let's not jump to conclusions
we don't know all the facts

                  This is not about race
         this is a time for mourning

Wait for the police statement
the Prime Minister's press conference

                    this is about us

                  Isn't she amazing

Stop using divisive language
this is a time for mourning

                    aren't we all

              The horror will eat us

Finger pointing will get us nowhere
why does everything have to be about race

             in our sleep if we let it

          Let us hold you and cry

He's not even from here
we are bigger than that

        our grief into your hijabs

          Who would have thought

We feel so awful that this would happen
in our beautiful little country

            you'd be the victim

                Isn't it so sad

We are so sorry you had to see that
this isn't what you came here for

        if only we said something

          Haven't you had enough

This isn't the New Zealand
we know and love

          time in the spotlight

         What more do you need

Please come and talk on our show tomorrow

no don't bring that up
        we are all in this together

        amen

THE PRIME MINISTER WILL NOT SAY HIS NAME BUT I WILL

Harry Potter taught me to speak evil out of hiding

say the name no one wants to

bleed the fear from the stump

I will practice saying it in a mirror

listen as my throat convulses

exaggerate its edges

stretch it with my tongue

I will teach it to my children

so they will recognise evil

when it greets them at the door

lips snarled and gun cocked

they will know a hatred by its name

/brenton

/tarrant

perhaps it is easier

to unspeak a horror

that doesn't look you in the eye

but I can't unseat a thunder

an angry rain that tears

a screaming flash of white

the sound of bullets

casing a carpet sea

a parish of linen bodies

marching to another life

the left of us holding

what rest we have

make no mistake

none of us think you a deity

a devil

or a wicked fool

we will say your name

until you are no more real

until your oblivion fades

and we will have sprouted

daffodils from our pain

a forest from our eyes

a mountain

a most beautiful way to heal

and who will worship you then?

THE SHINING

Every good boy knows to keep his mouth shut

keep his muzzle tight

keep his words to himself

                                        I am sorry

                                        I am sorry

                                        I am sorry

he will chalk his knuckles into the pavement

to choke out an unhinging

a puerile thought

that doesn't sound like his

inside the birds are flying in circles

it is a miracle of modern science

the fluorescent has stunned them into a halo

they think they are going home

they have never seen masculinity tearing its own lips

every good young man knows not to sing for dead boys

to bury them before they have been named

carry their musket eyes to battle

worship a foreign skin

that does not taste like his

I am here to save you

you are mine now

forgive me

every good man is tired from chasing his animal

is dancing in circles

is forgetting which way home is

is a currency of lust and anger

is man up and stupid boy

is motherless and full of fathers he can never drown

is waiting to see his name in lights

to hear it chanted by the masses

to line his pockets with mist

until steam is rising from his head

and he is smiling in fear

we will stare up at him and wonder

what it is like to be that holy

that absolute and still

and undeniably great

AOTEAROA INC.

God defend this lucky country
this bowl of furious blossom

a bosom of river and trees
and never looking back

how much we tease out
our accomplishments

drink beers from world cups
and hide the good whine

how easy do we hush
our groaning guts

our leaky family vans
eating away at us

the lush landscapes
we prefer not to disturb

God defend our crown enterprise

our Fontera hearts overflowing

with milk and manuka

and fertilizer and methane

God defend our coal mine catacombs

and small town charm offensive

spinning our yarns

over untouched secrets

God defend our suicidal youth

our tepid masculinity

our poppies slashed at the knees

lest we forgive ourselves

for ever climbing this high

ever reaching this far

ever knocking the bastard

off his hinges

God defend the Queen

and all her children

us drunken wife beaters

tucked into our gumboots

this tiny nation

that shakes the world

this quiet pride a flag

we hold in the stillness

no one has ever been

this authentically proud

THE GUEST HOUSE
for al Noor and Linwood

In this house

we have one rule:

> *bring only what you want*
>
> *to leave behind*

we open doors

with both hands

passing batons

from death to life

come share with us

this tiny peace

we built from broken tongues

and one-way boarding passes

from kauri bark

and scholarships

from kaitiaki

and kin

in this house

we are

                  all broken

                  all strange

                  all guests

we are holding

space for you

                  stranger

                  friend

come angry

come dazed

come hand against your frail

come open wounded

come heart between your knees

come sick and sleepless

come seeking shelter

come crawling in your lungs

come teeth inside your grief

come shattered peace

come foreign doubt

come unrequited sun

come shaken soil

come unbearable canyon

come desperately alone

come untuned blossom

come wild and hollow prayer

come celestial martyr

come singing doubt

come swimming to land

come weep

come whisper

come howl into embrace

come find

                           a new thread

                           a gentle light

                           a glass jar to hold

                                      your dust

come closer

come in

                           you are welcome, brother

NATIONAL ANTHEM

I pledge allegiance

> to love and good coffee
>
> a sleepy heart
>
> two sets of feet burning
>
> a clatter of brilliant voices
>
> raised as one

I pledge my honeycomb tongue

to the five stages of peace

> Anger
>
> Resilience
>
> Open palms
>
> History
>
> and New Beginnings

to broken and plastered hope

to our phoenix youth

our devils dancing in the wind

the ancient maps left for us

> to worship
>
> or forsake

I pledge a bowl of molasses

and my grandmothers laugh

to whoever will laugh with me

wrestle from the sun a hurricane

of Jinn stories and inside jokes

of multi-tongued monsters

finding homes in each other

I pledge myself to

no flag

no border

no house of trees

no fairytale past

no charismatic king

no industry of false profits

burying their dead in the sand

to them I only pledge

a steady voice

an untroubled heart

a desperate compassion

a fist raised in the air

to those who would plot to sow me love

to bake me warmth and never break my art

to rob my eyes for safe keeping

to drown me in unconditional trust

to build with me

a new sun

I pledge myself

to you

(UN)LEARNING MY NAME

/Mohamed/

/Moh.ham.ed/

/Mo...........haaaam.........ed/

the first time I am mistaken

for a white man I feel a rush

of joy / lurching from my gut

                    / a relief

I have finally won a place

a right to invisibility

                    / a belong

if only for a moment

a wicked pleasure that I have fit

so well in today / a passing thought

a comma on a blank page

                    / it doesn't last

I am asked what my name is

and I flinch / the jig is up

I am caught in a

                    / lie

                         /Moh.ham.ed/

the familiarity fades
a little flicker once lit
behind the eyes isn't
for me anymore

                    / the third stage of grief
                    is bargaining

    but you look so much like us   you don't look Arab at all
    where do you get your blue eyes from   they are so beautiful
it must be somewhere in your bloodline   we must be
        this beautiful   which parts of your ancestry
                do you owe us   which parts
                have you stolen
                /Moh.ham.ed/

I have spent my life
carving vowels
out of my throat
so my name will be

                    / easier to say

sanding down
my grandfather
so I could fit him in
a carry-on bag

a driver's license

a job interview

/Moh-ham-ed/

adjective: *praised one;*

thanked in the earth and sky;

I am pouring oil down my throat

until it lines my stomach

until no guttural could ever

/ escape

I still say it the way my first

white teacher said it

the way she corrected me

in front of the class

until I learnt how to stumble

/ over

/ my identity

/ the way

/ she did

how to strip away

parts of myself

that couldn't be marketed

to a Western

/ tongue

I still shave off my curly

hair and wear blue

to bring out my eyes

so beautiful!

where did they?

/Moh.ha.med/

/Moحa.mad/

/am.madحم/

it takes me nineteen years

to learn / how to pronounce

my own name

/ in public

 the first time I say it

the way my mother

did when she named me

/محمد/

it feels like I have

/ stolen

something back.

ACKNOWLEDGEMENTS

LAY OUT YOUR UNREST

www.ingramcontent.com/pod-product-compliance
Lightning Source LLC
Chambersburg PA
CBHW020212090426
42734CB00008B/1039